Bridgestone
BOOKS

Life in the World's Biomes

Desert Plants

by Catherine A. Welch

Consultant:
Ian A. Ramjohn, PhD
Department of Botany and Microbiology
University of Oklahoma
Norman, Oklahoma

Capstone
press

Mankato, Minnesota

Bridgestone Books are published by Capstone Press,
151 Good Counsel Drive, P.O. Box 669, Mankato, Minnesota 56002.
www.capstonepress.com

Library of Congress Cataloging-in-Publication Data
Welch, Catherine A.
    Desert plants / by Catherine A. Welch.
    p. cm.—(Bridgestone Books. Life in the world's biomes)
    Summary: "Describes desert plants, how desert plants are used, and why they need to be
protected"—Provided by publisher.
    Includes bibliographical references and index.
    ISBN 0-7368-4321-3 (hardcover)
    1. Desert plants—Juvenile literature. I. Title. II. Series: Life in the world's biomes.
QK938.D4W45 2006
581.7'54—dc22   2004028491

Editorial Credits
Amber Bannerman, editor; Jennifer Bergstrom, designer; Kelly Garvin, photo researcher;
    Scott Thoms, photo editor

Photo Credits
Art Directors/TRIP, 14
Brand X Pictures, 1
Bruce Coleman Inc./Frank Cara, 12
Corbis/B.S.P.I., cover; Darrell Gulin, 6 (left); L. Clarke, 18; Tom Bean, 8
Minden Pictures/Jim Brandenburg, 6 (bottom right)
Nature Picture Library/Neil Lucas, 20
Peter Arnold Inc./Lin Alder, 16
Steve Mulligan, 4
Tom Stack & Associates Inc./Doug Sokell, 6 (top right)
Visuals Unlimited/Rick and Nora Bowers, 10

The author thanks Judith Stark, Jacqueline Hoffman, and the staff of the Southbury, Connecticut,
library for their assistance in gathering material for this book.

Table of Contents

Deserts

Sand and rocks cover the ground. A spiny cactus stands tall. The weather is hot and dry. Is this how you picture a desert? Some deserts have these features, but others are very different.

Deserts are found all over the world. They can be hot or cold. Some deserts have mountains. Others have sand **dunes**. All deserts are very dry places. Most get less than 10 inches (25 centimeters) of rain or snow each year. All desert plants have found ways to live with little water.

◄ The giant barrel cactus can grow 10 feet (3 meters) tall.

Desert Plants

Many deserts are known for their **succulent** plants. These plants store water in stems, roots, and leaves. Cactuses are succulents.

Deserts are also homes for grasses, wildflowers, **shrubs**, and small trees. Some grasses, such as spinifex, are spiky and grow in clumps. Spinifex grows in the Australian desert. Wildflowers, like gold poppies, brighten deserts. Most desert shrubs grow low to the ground. Mesquite (muh-SKEET) shrubs and trees grow in the southwestern United States.

◄ The saguaro cactus (left), mesquite tree (top right), and gold poppies (bottom right) are a few of the many desert plants.

Desert Plant Features

Desert plants make the most of little rain. Some have shallow roots. They soak up rain from a wide area. Some leaves and roots get water from fog and **dew**.

Desert plants must store water as long as possible. The hot desert sun can cause water to **transpire** from plants. Succulents and other desert plants have waxy coatings. They **reflect** sunlight and stop water loss. Some plants, like brittlebush shrubs, prevent water loss by rolling up their leaves.

◄ Waxy agave plant leaves help water slide down to the plant's roots.

Plant Homes for Animals

Animals use desert plants for shelter and shade. Lizards live in the thick leaves of yucca plants. Grasshoppers hide in the shade of creosote (KREE-uh-soht) bushes. In Australia, pigeons hide in spinifex grass. Their feathers look like the grass blades.

The saguaro cactus is a desert home for birds. Owls and hawks nest on the cactus. Gila woodpeckers peck holes in the cactus stem. Some birds nest in these holes.

◄ The great horned owl does not make its own nest. It stays in the old nests of other animals.

Plant Foods for Animals

Desert animals get most of their water by eating plants. Birds and insects get water from the juicy red fruit of the saguaro cactus. After rainfall, cactuses grow large flowers. Insects, birds, and long-nosed bats suck the flowers' watery **nectar**.

Desert plants are food and water for a variety of other animals. Rodents dig up plant bulbs and search for seeds. Ants store seeds in underground nests. In North America, bighorn sheep eat yucca and the leafy brittlebush.

◀ Cactus wrens use their long beaks to eat fruit and drink nectar.

Plants Used by People

Desert plants are useful for people as well as animals. Cooks make the pink fruit of the hedgehog cactus into jam. Fruit of the organ-pipe cactus tastes like watermelon.

People also use parts of desert plants that can't be eaten. Parts of thick succulent leaves are used to make baskets, mats, ropes, and sandals. The woody trunk of the sagebrush burns well for campfires. In South America, some cactus spines are used as sewing needles.

◄ In Africa, weavers make mats from parts of desert plants.

Plants in Danger

Some desert plants are harmed by people and animals. Tires of off-road vehicles crush plants. People use plants for food and firewood. Animal herds often eat too many plants from one area of land. The yeheb nut bush has almost disappeared from African deserts because of overuse.

In Saudi Arabia, workers drill for oil beneath the desert ground. Sometimes oil spills. Desert plants cannot grow in oil-covered ground.

← Tracks show where a vehicle drove over plants in the Mojave desert.

Protecting Desert Plants

Desert plants must be protected. When plants are destroyed or taken, animals lose homes and food. Plants useful for medicines are also lost.

Today, many countries have laws and ways to help protect desert plants. People use special equipment to clean up oil spills in the desert. Some deserts are protected in national parks or conservation areas.

◄ Desert plants are protected in Uluru National Park in Australia.

The Amazing Birdcage Plant

Desert plants have many unusual ways to spread their seeds in dry climates. The birdcage plant is one. It gets its name from what happens after it dies.

The birdcage plant dies when wind uncovers the roots. The sun bakes the roots and causes the plant to dry and curl up. The plant then looks like a brown birdcage. Wind blows the dried plant. The plant tumbles across the desert, spilling its seeds. Some seeds find shady spots with dew. New birdcage plants then take root in the desert.

◄ The birdcage plant can travel miles across a desert.

Glossary

dew (DOO)—water in the form of small drops that collect overnight on cool surfaces outside

dune (DOON)—a sand hill made by wind

nectar (NEK-tur)—a sweet liquid in flowers

reflect (ri-FLEKT)—to bounce back light

shrub (SHRUHB)—a plant or bush with woody stems that branch out near the ground

succulent (SUHK-yuh-luhnt)—a plant with thick, fleshy leaves or stems that can store water; a cactus is a succulent.

transpire (tran-SPYE-ur)—to give off water; plants transpire through tiny holes in their leaves.

Read More

Cole, Melissa. *Deserts.* Wild America Habitats. San Diego: Blackbirch Press, 2003.

Wilkins, Sally. *Deserts.* The Bridgestone Science Library. Mankato, Minn.: Bridgestone Books, 2001.

Internet Sites

FactHound offers a safe, fun way to find Internet sites related to this book. All of the sites on FactHound have been researched by our staff.

Here's how:
1. Visit *www.facthound.com*
2. Type in this special code **0736843213** for age-appropriate sites. Or enter a search word related to this book for a more general search.
3. Click on the **Fetch It** button.

FactHound will fetch the best sites for you!

Index